Fact Finders™

The American Colonies

The Virginia Colony

by Brandy Bauer

Consultant:
Julie Richter
Consultant, Colonial Williamsburg Foundation
Williamsburg, Virginia

Capstone
press

Mankato, Minnesota

Fact Finders is published by Capstone Press,
151 Good Counsel Drive, P.O. Box 669, Mankato, Minnesota 56002.
www.capstonepress.com

Library of Congress Cataloging-in-Publication Data
Bauer, Brandy.
   The Virginia colony / by Brandy Bauer.
   p. cm.—(Fact Finders. The American colonies)
   Includes bibliographical references and index.
   ISBN 0-7368-2684-X (hardcover)
   1. Virginia—History—Colonial period, ca. 1600–1775—Juvenile literature. I. Title. II.
Series: Fact Finders. The American colonies (Capstone Press)
F229.B34 2006
975.5'02—dc22
                                              2004029075

Summary: An introduction to the history, government, economy, resources, and people of
the Virginia Colony. Includes maps and charts.

Editorial Credits
Katy Kudela, editor; Jennifer Bergstrom, set designer, illustrator, and book designer;
   Bobbi J. Dey, book designer; Wanda Winch, photo researcher/photo editor

Photo Credits
Cover image: Tobacco production in Jamestown, National Parks Service/Colonial National
   Historical Park

Capstone Press Archives, 22
Corbis/Bettmann, 4–5
The Granger Collection, New York, 18, 20–21, 26, 27
Image courtesy of Virginia Fry, 13
National Archives and Records Administration, 29 (right)
National Parks Service/Colonial National Historical Park, 6, 10, 16–17, 29 (left)
North Wind Picture Archives, 7, 11, 14
Photri-Microstock, 23

1 2 3 4 5 6 10 09 08 07 06 05

Table of Contents

Chapter 1

Virginia's First People

The Virginia Colony was built on land first settled by the American Indians. The Indians had lived there for thousands of years. The Monacan and Manahoac lived in the western part of what became Virginia. They hunted and gathered food in the many forests. The Susquehanna farmed and fished in the northern part of the Chesapeake Bay. The Cherokee farmed and hunted in the mountains.

Powhatan Indians

The Powhatan Indians were one of the largest groups in Virginia. Chief Powhatan ruled this group of 30 tribes. These tribes formed the Powhatan Chiefdom.

English settlers recognized
Chief Powhatan as the leader
of the Powhatan Indians.

The Powhatan lived off the land.
They hunted deer and gathered
nuts. They grew corn and other crops.

Settlers Arrive

In 1607, English settlers sailed to what
is now Virginia. The Indians were uneasy
about the settlers' arrival. The Powhatan
didn't want the settlers to ruin their
chiefdom and land.

The American
Indians watched
as the English
settled in Virginia.
The Indians were
worried the settlers
would take all of
the land. ▼

The Powhatan were the first to meet with the English settlers in Virginia. At first, they did not trust the English. They tried to keep the English off their land. Over time, the Powhatan accepted the English settlers. They gave the settlers food. They also taught the settlers how to live on the land. This friendly relationship lasted only a few years. Soon, the settlers began to take the American Indians' land.

▲ The Powhatan Indians learned to get along with the English settlers living in Virginia.

FACT!

Pocahontas, the daughter of Chief Powhatan, helped save the Virginia settlers. She brought them food when they were starving.

Chapter 2

Early Settlers

The first European settlers in Virginia were English. They arrived in ships owned by the Virginia Company of London. The company hoped to find gold and silver in the area.

Just over 100 men and boys were on board the ships. Many of the settlers agreed to work for the Virginia Company. In exchange, they received food and a chance to own land.

After four months at sea, the settlers arrived in North America. They built a settlement called Jamestown, named after King James I of England. The king had given the Virginia Company a **grant** for land in North America.

Jamestown was the first settlement in the Virginia Colony. By 1763, Virginia's borders included a larger area. ➤

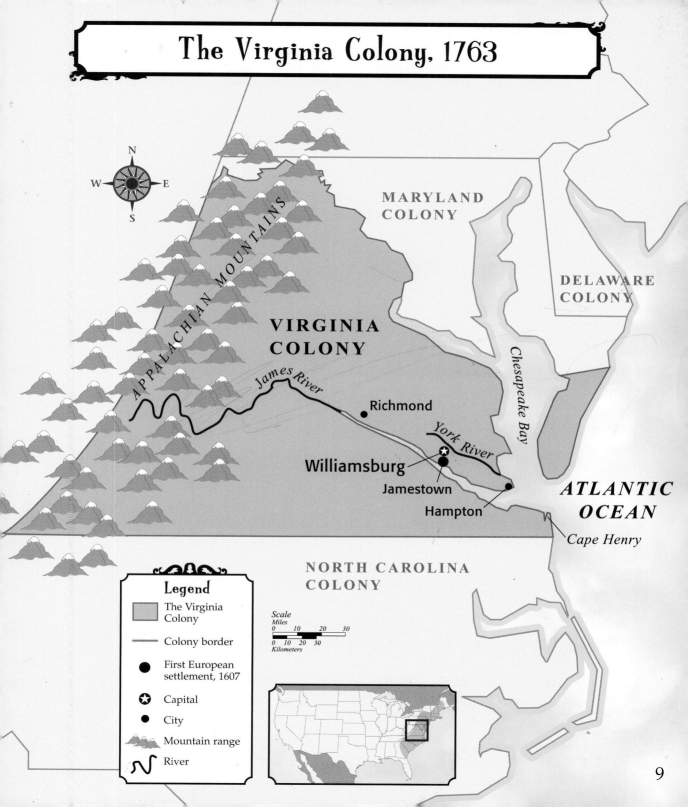

The Virginia Colony, 1763

MARYLAND COLONY

DELAWARE COLONY

VIRGINIA COLONY

APPALACHIAN MOUNTAINS

James River

Richmond

York River

Chesapeake Bay

Williamsburg

Jamestown

Hampton

ATLANTIC OCEAN

Cape Henry

NORTH CAROLINA COLONY

N W E S

Legend

The Virginia Colony

Colony border

First European settlement, 1607

Capital

City

Mountain range

River

Scale
Miles
0   10   20   30
0 10 20 30
Kilometers

Jamestown was the first permanent English colony in North America.

Building a Colony

Jamestown's first settlers struggled to survive. Many settlers were wealthy men in England. They did not know how to farm. Only 38 settlers survived the first year.

In 1608, a new group of settlers and supplies arrived. But Jamestown's supplies didn't last. Between 1609 and 1610, a drought ruined the colony's crops. The settlers ran out of food. Many starved to death.

The colony struggled into the 1620s. Many settlers died from **malaria**. Others were killed in battles with the Powhatan.

The settlers' relationship with the Powhatan often changed. Sometimes the two groups traded goods with each other. Other times, they fought over land.

These troubles did not stop the colony's growth. The surviving settlers took land for **plantations**. By the 1640s, the Powhatan had lost most of their land. In 1646, the Virginia settlers and the Powhatan signed a peace treaty. The treaty placed the Powhatan on small pieces of land called reservations.

▲ The Powhatan grew angry as the English settlers continued to take their land.

FACT!

Legend holds that Captain John Smith helped save Jamestown from starvation. Smith learned to speak and trade with the Powhatan.

Chapter 3

Colonial Life

As the Virginia Colony grew, the colonists' houses changed. During the early years, the colonists built homes from pine and oak trees. Most people lived in one-room houses.

By the 1700s, some Virginia colonists had grown wealthy. They built larger homes. In the capital city of Williamsburg, some houses were built of brick. The richest families lived in mansions. These houses had many rooms. The mansions also had libraries with books from England.

The settlers in Jamestown lived in wood houses with thatched roofs.

During the colony's early years, many people did not have enough food to eat. ▼

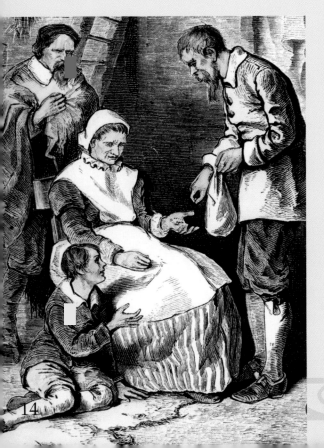

Food

In the early years, the Jamestown settlers ate what they could find. They ate mainly fish, turtles, and corn. Settlers often grew weak from hunger.

As more people came to Virginia, they brought food supplies with them. People also learned to grow food.

Colonial Schools

The colony had few schools. Some rich colonists sent their children to school in England. Other wealthy families hired tutors.

In colonial times, boys often received more schooling than girls. Boys learned to read and write. They also studied math, history, Greek, and Latin. Some girls also learned to read and write. But most girls learned to cook, sew, and take care of the home.

Population Growth of the Virginia Colony

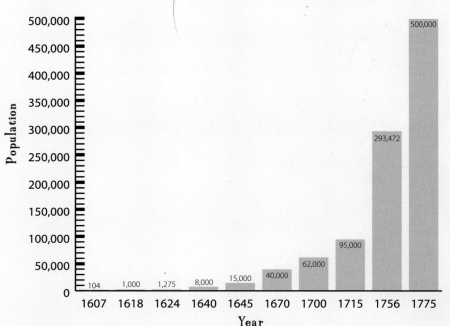

~ Chapter 4 ~
Work and Trade

In 1612, colonist John Rolfe brought new tobacco seeds to Virginia. The seeds came from the West Indies. Rolfe's tobacco grew well in Virginia's soil. Tobacco quickly became the colony's biggest crop.

The demand for Virginia's tobacco grew. Planters soon needed help to grow the crop. In 1619, a Dutch ship came to Virginia with about 20 Africans on board. These were the first Africans to come to Virginia. The colonists put the Africans to work on their plantations. Historians do not know how these Africans were treated. They may have been viewed as servants or even owned as slaves.

Virginia farmers shipped barrels of tobacco to England.

As plantations grew, the colony needed more workers. **Indentured servants** were often poor men and women who could not find work in England. Many worked on Virginia plantations for a fixed number of years. After their term was done, they were free to leave.

By the end of the 1600s, Virginia planters used slaves instead of indentured servants. Slaves were shipped from Africa to work for the colonists. Slaves worked many hours in the tobacco fields for no pay.

Many plantation owners used slaves to work in their tobacco fields. ▼

Tobacco

The tobacco growing season lasted nearly all year. In January, slaves and farmers prepared the fields. They planted the seeds in spring. In fall, the colonists harvested the tobacco and shipped it to England.

Tobacco sold well in England. By 1660, the colonists in Virginia had sent 10 million pounds (4.5 million kilograms) of tobacco to England. Tobacco brought wealth to Virginia and other southern colonies.

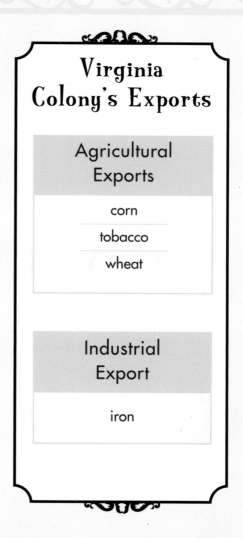

Virginia Colony's Exports

Agricultural Exports

corn

tobacco

wheat

Industrial Export

iron

Chapter 5

Community and Faith

King James I of England was the leader of the Virginia Colony. But as the ruler of England, he could not easily control the colony's daily business. In 1619, King James I created a local government called the House of Burgesses.

Members of the House of Burgesses met with Virginia's governor and his council. They helped make <u>laws</u> for the colony. Members also created **taxes** to pay for the colony's government.

The colonists in Virginia paid more than just government taxes. They paid taxes to support their churches. They also paid taxes on goods from England.

Members of the House of Burgesses helped create laws for the Virginia Colony.

▲ Each of the American colonies had its own paper currency. In Virginia, it was common for people to pay their taxes with tobacco.

By the mid-1700s, many colonists were tired of paying taxes to Great Britain. People were also angry over the Navigation Acts. These British laws stopped the colonies from trading with other countries. Colonists decided they wanted to make their own laws. They also wanted to choose their own **representatives** in Great Britain's government.

FACT!

Virginia law made people go to church at least once a month. The fine for not going was 50 pounds (23 kilograms) of tobacco.

Changing Religions

By the 1750s, many colonists no longer supported the Church of England. They wanted to follow other religions.

Baptist and Methodist preachers began to travel through Virginia. Some settlers found they preferred the teachings of these religions.

Virginia colonists gathered for Sunday service at the Bruton Parish Church in Williamsburg. ▼

Chapter 6

Becoming a State

By the mid-1700s, Virginia's population had grown to nearly 230,000. The colony was crowded. Virginia colonists began to look for new land for their plantations. Colonists moved north along the rivers and into the Appalachian Mountains.

The colonists were not the only people looking for new land. Both the British and French wanted to control more land in North America. In 1754, British soldiers came to Virginia. They fought the French for control of land west of the colonies. The French and Indian War lasted until 1763.

Virginia was the first of the 13 colonies. In 1763, the colony borders were set. ➡

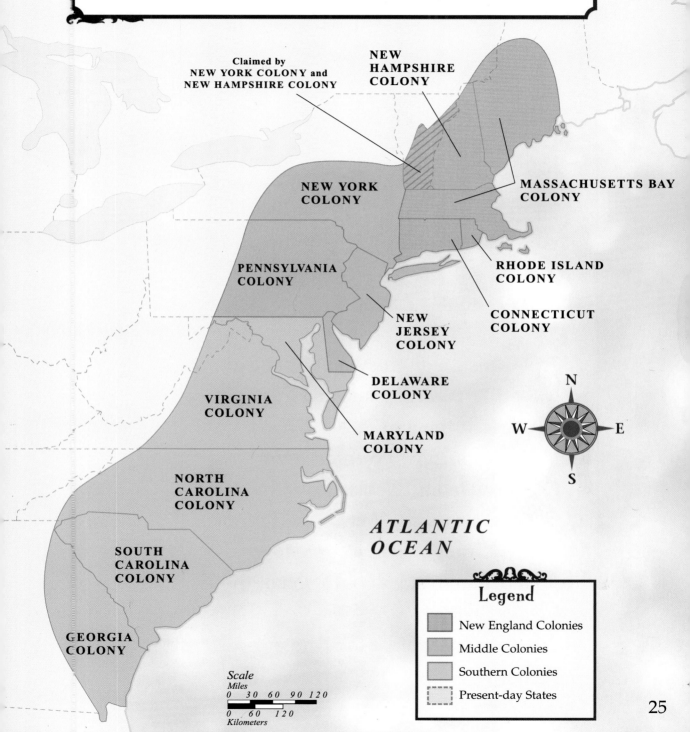

The Thirteen Colonies, 1763

Claimed by
NEW YORK COLONY and
NEW HAMPSHIRE COLONY

NEW
HAMPSHIRE
COLONY

NEW YORK
COLONY

MASSACHUSETTS BAY
COLONY

PENNSYLVANIA
COLONY

RHODE ISLAND
COLONY

NEW
JERSEY
COLONY

CONNECTICUT
COLONY

DELAWARE
COLONY

VIRGINIA
COLONY

MARYLAND
COLONY

N
W   E
S

NORTH
CAROLINA
COLONY

*ATLANTIC
OCEAN*

SOUTH
CAROLINA
COLONY

GEORGIA
COLONY

Scale
Miles
0   30   60   90   120
0   60   120
Kilometers

Legend

New England Colonies
Middle Colonies
Southern Colonies
Present-day States

25

The British won the war, but at a
great cost. To pay for the war, Great
Britain passed the Stamp Act. This act
taxed the colonists on printed items.

Colonists in all 13 colonies were
angry with the Stamp Act. They did not
want to pay more taxes. People in
Virginia began to speak out. One of these
men was Patrick Henry. He asked others
to take up arms against the British.

In 1774, the colonies sent representatives to the Continental Congress. They discussed what the colonies should do about Great Britain.

The following year, the first battle of the Revolutionary War (1775–1783) broke out. This began the colonies' fight for freedom.

In July 1776, Congress announced the United States' independence with the Declaration of Independence. But Britain refused to give up its control. The United States finally won the war in 1783.

On June 25, 1788, Virginia approved the U.S. **Constitution**. It was the 10th state to join the United States.

⬆ Thomas Jefferson of Virginia, second from left, wrote most of the Declaration of Independence.

Fast Facts

Name
The Virginia Colony

Location
Southern colonies

Year of Founding
1607

First Settlement
Jamestown

Colony's Founders
Settlers sent by the Virginia Company of London

Religious Faiths
Anglican, Baptist, Methodist

Agricultural Product
Tobacco

Major Industry
Tobacco

Population in 1775
500,000 people

Statehood
June 25, 1788 (10th state)

Time Line

1619
King James I forms a local government for Virginia called the House of Burgesses.

1612
John Rolfe brings new tobacco seeds to Virginia; tobacco becomes the colony's main crop.

1607
Englishmen arrive in present-day Virginia; they build Jamestown Fort.

1707
An Act of Union unites England, Wales, and Scotland; they become the Kingdom of Great Britain.

1754-1763
British soldiers come to North America to fight the French and Indian War.

1763
Proclamation of 1763 sets colonial borders and provides land for American Indians.

1774
First Continental Congress meets in Philadelphia.

1776
Declaration of Independence is approved in July.

1775-1783
American colonists and the British fight the Revolutionary War.

1788
On June 25, Virginia is the 10th state to join the United States.

29

Glossary

constitution (kon-stuh-TOO-shuhn)—the system of written laws in a state or country that state the rights of the people and the powers of the government

grant (GRANT)—a gift such as land or money given for a particular purpose

indentured servant (in-DEN-churd SUR-vuhnt)—someone who agrees to work for another person for a certain length of time in exchange for travel expenses, food, housing, and clothing

malaria (muh-LAIR-ee-ah)—a serious disease that people get from mosquito bites

plantation (plan-TAY-shun)—a large farm where crops such as coffee, tea, tobacco, and cotton are grown

representative (rep-ri-ZEN-tuh-tiv)—someone who is chosen to speak or act for others

tax (TAKS)—money collected from a country's citizens to help pay for running the government

Internet Sites

FactHound offers a safe, fun way to find Internet sites related to this book. All of the sites on FactHound have been researched by our staff.

Here's how:

1. Visit *www.facthound.com*
2. Type in this special code **073682684X** for age-appropriate sites. Or enter a search word related to this book for a more general search.
3. Click on the **Fetch It** button.

FactHound will fetch the best sites for you!

Read More

De Capua, Sarah. *The Virginia Colony.* Our Thirteen Colonies. Chanhassen, Minn.: Child's World, 2004.

Glaser, Jason. *Patrick Henry: Liberty or Death.* Graphic Library. Graphic Biographies. Mankato, Minn. Capstone Press, 2006.

Sonneborn, Liz. *Pocahontas, 1595–1617.* American Indian Biographies. Mankato, Minn.: Blue Earth Books, 2003.

Index